The Process of Change

A Look at Me: Volume One

Precious Brown

Flint Michigan

The Process of Change
A Look at Me: Volume One
Copyright © 2015 by Precious Brown

All rights are reserved. Except as permitted under the U.S. Copyright Act of 1976, no part of the publication may be reproduced, distributed or transmitted in any form or by any means, or stored in a database or retrieval system without the prior written permission of the publisher.

This book is available in volume for qualifying organizations. Please contact the author to inquire.
code@changenegative2positive.com

For more information about this book, coaching, or speaking engagements please visit www.changenegative2positive.com or email code@changenegative2positive.com.

KILGORE PUBLISHING
Flint Michigan
Since 2015

ISBN 978-0996134712
For Worldwide Distribution
Printed in the U.S.A

Contents

Dedication
Introduction

1. Life Events
2. Impact
3. Where will I start?
4. Supporters
5. *ME* Time
6. After Quiet Time
7. Perception
8. Who am I?
9. Letting Go
10. Goals
11. Turning Point
12. Affirmations
13. Bonus

Dedication

I dedicate this book to the Loves of my life; God and my children.

I thank God every day for a new life and a second chance to live it according to His will. It is only by His grace and mercy that I am sober with a sound mind. As such, I am willing and able to create this workbook for the betterment of His people. I believe it is His will for me to share my testimonies so others will be freed from bondage.

To my children I thank you for loving me in spite of me and through it all. You are my inspiration and I am proud of all of you in every stage of your lives. I am astonished at the productive adults you are becoming.

Although, life is not perfect (nor will it ever be) know that there will always be trials and tribulations and with prayer you can make it through them.

Be mindful and learn from your mistakes. Make a conscious decision to make better choices and become a better you. Always remember Mommy loves you all.

Introduction

One definition of change is to make the form, nature, content, or future course of something different from what it is or from what it would be if left alone. The simplest definition is: to make or become different.

This workbook will assist you in implementing a change process in your life so you can become a **better you**. *Note* this is not going to be as easily practiced as it sounds on paper. Be prepared to have a whirlwind of thoughts and emotions. Be wise enough to step back from the process for a day or so (no more than that) if it becomes too much; but you must come back to it and be dedicated to changing you. **Change is needed for growth.**

You have taken a brave and needed step in your life. I applaud you for beginning your change process. As such it is necessary for you to write. This workbook was created to assist you with journaling your thoughts. Embrace this new adventure and watch the new you unfold.

The Process of Change

Before you read any further I would like to say Thank You for your support it is an honor to have you read this book. It is important that you understand the information you will read is not scripted. Every word written is from my heart. It is a compilation of events throughout my life. It is intended to assist you with your life change process. I chose this method of writing so you fully understand – I was able to change and **you are able to change**.

With the help of God, and two of my dearest friends, I was fortunate enough be able to conquer some tough issues and make some serious changes in my life, without intensive counseling. My prayer is for you to see yourself as a diamond in the rough.

Believe in your heart, by the end of your journey, you will be shiny and polished. I pray the workbook inspires you to work through your change process, by looking deep within, and stay the course.

Journal Writings to become a better you!

You have purchased this workbook because you have decided you need something done differently in your life. You may have tried several self-help books or this may be your first; either way **Congratulations, you made the right choice**. This is your first step to changing your life forever.

The hardest thing for many of us to do is change but it can be done. As humans we want everyone and everything around us to change, but in order for that to happen, we must change ourselves. We must take a long hard look at ourselves. This is not the superficial look such as looking in the mirror; but the look deep within; identifying what makes us tick and why.

Self-reflection allows you to identify the issues of your life. It gives you an idea of how you have become the person you are today. You must deal with all of your issues to truly change on the inside.

Granted, some issues may take longer to reach and may be more difficult to deal with, but you must confront every one of them. There is no minimum or maximum amount of time in which you will see the magnificent change in yourself, however, if you are consistent and honest you will begin to change!!!

At any point you decide you need a professional to assist you; please get that help!

Writing #1

Life Events

As a young girl I was abused, in different manners, by several people I trusted. I never told or dealt with it. In turn, I internalized everything. As a teenager I was defiant, violent and very promiscuous. I began to date a much older boy and eventually, he began to physically abuse me. It went on for about a year; in secret. I was afraid to tell my parents because they previously told me not to see him. None of my friends knew the full story of our relationship. I believed they would have thought I was stupid. They would not understand I could not leave because I was terrified of him. So, I suffered in silence. The hold he had on me was released when he was sent to prison for killing one of my classmates. After he was gone I was able to refocus on my studies and graduate from high school.

In my late teens I had my first child. Soon after I met my first husband. During the 16 years we were together it was a nonstop rollercoaster. I completely lost myself and hadn't even noticed I was gone. In the midst, there was emotional and verbal abuse, health issues and many other things going on. At some point, there was a disconnect from the children. I engaged in heavy drugs and alcohol for several years. I rationalized and gave excuses as to why- such as hoping to keep the relationship together or it made me feel good, or I just needed an escape; Boy was I wrong! The truth was I did not want to deal with what was happening around me.

Through it all I managed to have a decent paying job, halfway raise my children and keep a somewhat stable home. On the outside we seemed to be the normal all American family; Dad, Mom and four children (two girls and two boys) but on the inside we were as dysfunctional as a computer with a virus.

The facade of our lives erupted on a hot summer day, August 8, 2008. That was the day he tried to kill me. He put a loaded gun to my chest and pulled the trigger.

I thank God, every day, the gun jammed. Needless to say it was the end of the marriage. I was desperately holding on to life itself. **I had no direction, ambition, or motivation. I was lost**. I felt I had no need to keep living. I had no idea it would be the worst and best day of my life; the beginning of my change process.

It has taken six long years to reach the point of writing this workbook. I have changed drastically. I have grown, healed and learned a lot. My oldest three children are productive adults. The fourth child will graduate from high school in 2015. I have three wonderful grandsons and a grand-daughter on the way. I am living and loving life with as little strife as possible. I am humbly thankful to God every day.

Throughout life there may have been several events that impacted you in many different ways.

Write about two events that have impacted your life negatively.

_____

_____

_____

_____

_____

_____

_____

_____

_____

_____

_____

_____

_____

_____

_____

_____

Writing #2

IMPACT

Write the lessons you learned from the two experiences you described on the previous page.

Writing # 3

Where Will I start?

There may be multiple areas of your life affected at the same time. It is highly suggested you try to concentrate on one area at a time. Please gauge yourself; try not to get overwhelmed and decide to quit the process. **Quitting should not be an option**. Remember this change may be hard to you but it is for your good.

Many people want to change on the inside but do not have a clue where to start. I was the same way. I had to figure it out and with God's help; I did.

I suggest you start with the issue in your life that is easiest for you to deal with at this time. Each issue may cause you to have different thoughts and emotions. Before starting this process **there are several important things to remember to be successful:**

Always be honest with yourself. Sugarcoating any area that is uncovered will only set you up for failure – no one knows you like you and no one can change you but you!

I must admit when I began to deal with the issues of my life it was overwhelming. It seemed as though the pain would never end. I started having flash memories of things I had suppressed. I had to face the fact I was getting a divorce. I had to deal with my children rebelling. I was working 10-12 hours every day. In the midst, I became a functioning alcoholic. I woke up drinking with my coffee. If I could I would drink on lunch. When I got home I was definitely had a few drinks; if not an entire bottle.

A friend called it to my attention often but I would dismiss it by saying "I don't drink that much". I started masking the alcohol in juice bottles or pop bottles to make it appear as if I was not drinking. I was forced to be honest with myself and deal with my drinking when I almost got fired. One Monday I overslept well into the afternoon. I had been drinking from

Wednesday to Sunday and didn't notice it. When I woke up that Monday my children had missed school and I had missed work. Since it was about 1p.m. I was considered a no call no show. I had to practically beg not to be fired. I was put on 60 day probation at work. I had never been so disgusted with myself in my life. Had I been honest and addressed the drinking issue months earlier, when my friend asked about it, I could have saved myself the embarrassment. I began the process of overcoming alcoholism on that day.

Be committed to deal with old and new wounds in your life regardless of who or what it involves. Over the last years I have begun to deal with a new aspect of my change process – being able to forgive. I had deep hurts regarding my parents for various reasons. I had not been willing to deal with the hurts nor my parents. At times I would go without speaking to them for weeks at a time. It was easier to not talk than to possibly scrape the scab off an old wound.

However, I knew at some point I would have to address the issues or I could never fully heal my heart. Talking with either of my parents, about my feelings, was not an easy task but it had to be done. Reluctantly and prayerfully I addressed some issues with each of them. After the communication took place I was able to have closure and move on.

Be willing to step away from anyone or anything that hinders your positive change process – this could be family, friends, or a situation at work or school - please use discretion. There was a time during the early parts of my process I allowed myself to fall prey to other people. I had a couple of close acquaintances and we decided to do a trial run of a business.

We worked on the details for a couple months and then launched. During the first event I quickly learned one of the partners was in for herself. It came out that she was stealing from the business and I was very angry. Almost immediately I noticed my anger and decided I would confront the issue.

Not in a combative manner; more matter-of-factly. To be sure I would not allow myself to fall back into my old ways of fighting, backbiting, gossiping or hatred I decided it was best to disconnect from the source.

Currently we are cordial but that is the extent of the acquaintanceship. *Note* - if you cannot remove the obstacle permanently or completely discontinue contact until you are strong enough to deal with the obstacle and your process at the same time.

Pay attention to you! Acknowledge your feelings, your triggers and your reactions. Use your journal to write them down to get familiar with them. For example, when you get angry ask yourself - why did that upset me so much? Questioning your emotions will allow you to acknowledge your triggers. Then you will learn to deal with things before they happen not after your reaction.

When I decided to move forward with my change process I made a conscious effort to get to know me.

I began to realize I was angry all the time and I had no idea why. One day my son, who was 7 or 8 at the time, was making a sandwich and neglected to wipe the counter off after he finished. When I saw it I immediately began to yell and fuss at him. Later that day I reflected on the situation to understand why I was so angry about a few crumbs on the counter.

I realized it had nothing to do with the crumbs. It had everything to do with my expectation of him cleaning up the way I would after making a sandwich. I also realized I never shared my expectation with him. He had no idea of the real issue. I explained to him after making a sandwich next time he was required to clean the counter. Thankfully we have not had that issue since.

Although this example was not an extreme issue. I was able to recognize the trigger of my anger and dealt with it immediately.

Since that time I have been able to recognize when I am allowing something, big or small, to make me angry and I consciously deal with it right away.

There may be several issues you can address right now but you must have a starting point.

What is the first change you want to make and why?

_____

_____

_____

_____

_____

_____

_____

_____

Writing #4

Supporters

Get a Positive support system. Drop the negative. My first of many attempts to stop using cocaine was an eye opener to my support system. When I seriously wanted to stop using this drug I shared the thought with my partner in crime. Instantly, he agreed it was a good idea. He assured me he would help me stop. He vowed to no longer supply it or do it around me. However, the assistance was short lived. **Be advised a junkie can't help a junkie quit anything no matter how hard they try!**

Truth is, I didn't want any of my friends or other family to know – what would they think of me? One day after partaking in the use of cocaine at work, I knew I was addicted and only God could help me.

I got on my knees in the stall and began to pray. I asked God to help me stop. From that day forward I pleaded with God to take the cravings away, but He didn't. I felt He was silent.

Fighting the addiction was causing turmoil in my spirit. I knew if the cocaine addiction could be broken, I could stand up and fight the rest of the demons in my life.

Out of desperation I told one of my best friends a little of what was going on. I knew she would not criticize, judge or look down her nose at me to make me feel lower than I already did. She assured me she would be with me through the quitting process. We prayed together often. I was able to call her when I the cravings surfaced or when I felt I was being pressured to do it.

After a while, I deliberately found other things to do to fill my drug time. As a result, I began to get stronger and stronger. Having someone positive to help me reinforce my long lost morals and values was key to my success. I thank her for that every day. The support system you have may make or break your change process. **Watch out for change killers.**

We all need positive supporters in our lives.

Write the names and phone numbers of 2-4 people who will support and encourage you through your change process.

_____

_____

_____

_____

_____

_____

_____

_____

_____

_____

_____

_____

*Contact your supporters, request their help and let them know what you are doing.

NOTE: different supporters may help you in different areas; not all will help at once or on the same issue(s). **

Writing # 5

ME Time
Meditation, Prayer or Quiet Time

We are all spiritual beings. **Your spiritual life is going to be an important tool throughout this process.** It is necessary to get in touch with your inner spirit so you are able to deal with suppressed issues. You must believe it in your heart, mind, and soul you are ready to change so your process will not be halted. You must decide to be mentally free. This will allow you to open up and tear down the protective walls you have unconsciously created.

Having quiet time will sustain you when the issues of your life seem to never stop raging. This is your "*me*" time. This is time away from everything and everybody. Time where you can think about nothing but you. Get in a closet if you must.

During this time, on occasion, you may find yourself crying, screaming, talking to yourself out loud or just sitting in silence. Whatever allows you to dig deep, do it! You will need this time more than ever. **Remember, when going through this process,** you must remain thankful for past and present experiences. The experiences had to take place for you change into the person you will be. Be thankful when things are going smoothly and especially when it gets rough. It's the rough times that things are changing the most.

 I chose prayer as my source to reach my inner spirit. Prayer is my free wireless communication with GOD! It allowed me to get to know and understand me on different levels. During my quiet time I realized I never knew what made me happy, sad or mad. It was in these times I began to realize just how confused I was about everything in my life.

  One of the hardest things to do when you are trying to make a change is to get some quiet time. There will be every interruption and excuse on planet earth as to why you cannot connect with your spirit. Make a choice and the sacrifice to dig deep within so you are successful in implementing your change.

Stop allowing excuses and interruptions to control the better you that is waiting to emerge.

It is important to get your "*ME*" time throughout this process. This will be when you connect with your inner spirit via meditation, prayer or quiet time.

Below write the time and place you will routinely have your quiet time.

_____

_____

_____

_____

_____

_____

_____

_____

_____

_____

_____

Writing #6

After quiet time

Write what you learned about yourself during your quiet time.

_____

_____

_____

_____

_____

_____

_____

_____

_____

_____

_____

_____

_____

you may repeat this journal step as often as you want

Writing #7

Is your perception correct?

Your perception is your vantage point of an issue or situation. We all have our own perceptions of how things are said to us, what certain things mean, how someone has treated us and so on.

However, perception is not always reality. It will be very important, when implementing your change process, you are careful not to dwell on your perception of any situation or person. You could be wrong. The saying *"things are not what they seem"* will come alive when you begin to change the way you think and act. At any time your perception is unclear, and it involves another person, **get clarification immediately**.

Do not ponder on your thoughts too longer before addressing issues; take immediate action. This will prevent more issues from arising or issues not being resolved. However, sometimes your perception is right and if that is the case, stand up for what you believe.

As I began to routinely utilize my prayer time it became evident I was angry with my father based on my perception of things he had done or said. I believed that he left me in a venerable situation as child and it caused a huge riff in our relationship. Due to this belief I did not effectively communicate with him about how I felt or why I felt that way. I was bitter on many levels. All because of how I perceived our relationship. When I began the forgiving stage of my change process I realized *things were not what they seemed*.

Once I opened up and allowed us to have a full heart to heart talk, via letter and phone calls, I understood that some of the things I perceived just were not true. I now understand he does love me. Although, I was right about some things; so was he. We are now working on having a better relationship and it is great!

There will be times when there is no clear cut right or wrong to your perception. At times such as these agree to disagree and move on. My husband and I have interesting conversations about any topic you can imagine. In the latest conversation we were discussing religious denominations and teachings. We are both raised in Baptist Churches but have different views on attending ***regularly***.

After a while of going back and forth about how often we should be attending church we had to come to a decision to agree to disagree and move on.

My perception is the more we attend the more we learn. I feel we should attend more services, such as Bible Study, Sunday morning and evening services. His perception is God is good with us being there on Sunday mornings. Although neither of us are wrong because there is no scriptural basis as to how many services we should attend; we agreed to disagree. This decision saved us from getting angry and in an argument and neither of us will change our way of thinking.

If you ever come to a point where you are aware that your perception is wrong accept it, apologize and move on. We are all wrong at some point in life.

This step is hard; but when you can do it you will know how much you are changing.

It is human error to have misperceptions. The issue comes when we act on what we perceive versus what actually happened.

Write about an incident where your perception was unclear.

_____

_____

_____

_____

_____

_____

_____

_____

_____

_____

_____

_____

Continued

What did you do to clarify your perception on the previous issue? If you have not done anything to clarify; what **WILL** you do?

_____

_____

_____

_____

_____

_____

_____

_____

_____

_____

_____

_____

_____

_____

Writing #8

Who Am I?

    This step in the change process is one of the most difficult. You may have no idea who you are in regards to what makes you tick. I know I had no idea who I was, what I wanted or how to figure it out. I didn't know what I enjoyed, what made me laugh or cry, what I wanted out of my career, or what I expected in a relationship.

    I had to take inventory of me. I ask you to do the same. It's okay that you have made mistakes in your life. You may make more while trying to figure *you* out. Accept errors with open arms. Learn from them and keep moving. Accept you for who you are, where you are, and allow your change to take place.

    This step will also give insight as to how you want to tackle your personal changes and issues that may arise.

Before I seriously started my change process I realized I had put all my dreams and goals on the back burner to be everything to everyone else. I no longer knew what direction I wanted to go in my professional or educational life; I was just making it. In 2002, in the midst of all the madness, I decided I wanted to continue my education. I enrolled in college and completed my Associates Degree in Business. It was a great milestone for me but my spirit wanted more.

I had a great sense of un-fulfillment but I didn't know what to do. I became even more frustrated and angry. I had been angry for so long I thought that was who I was; a mean lady.

I started finding and longing for more quiet time. During my quiet time one day, on my back porch, I began to ask myself questions like "what do you like?", "why are you angry all the time?", "how are you going to get past this point in life?"

Once I started to answer these questions honestly I was able to start acknowledging my triggers of issues. I was able to recognize the behavior and work on correcting it by communicating with words versus body language or other unproductive measures.

For example, I noticed that every time someone came to my house without calling first, I would get irritated. I would be short and unpleasant. I never recognized what I was doing until one of my girlfriends stopped by un-expectantly. This was not uncommon for her because she is like a sister to me.

However, this particular day my demeanor changed and she instantly noticed it. When she asked me what was wrong I said "nothing" with a snap. In that instant, the way she looked at me, made me realize something was off. I asked her "do I do that all the time?" She said "with other people, never with me."

I couldn't believe I had been doing it to others and no one brought it to my attention. Together we started dissecting my issue. First, I asked myself "why was I so irritated by her stopping by without calling?" Since she already told me I didn't normally do that to her, just to other people I needed to understand why. After we discussed it awhile I realized I felt that it was invading my privacy to have "*drop bys*". I felt the least someone could do was call before they came to my house, in case I did not want to have company at that time.

Going forward, I advised everyone to call before coming to my house. That simple piece of communication has allowed me to not have an attitude about something so miniscule in life.

To get to know who you are you must take inventory of your character and emotions.

Write five situations that make you happy, mad and sad and why.

_____

_____

_____

_____

_____

_____

Writing #9

Letting Go

You want to change for a reason. To fully change your old behavior and habits you must take ownership of your part in any situation. Granted, you cannot be held responsible for anything done to you as a child – which does directly affect who you are as an adult. However, you can own your actions, as an adult - which may have been derived from childhood pains. At some point you will have to give up all the "woe is me" attitudes, stop feeling sorry for yourself and having pity parties so that you can become whole. I get it, things were not the best for you. Guess what, it wasn't the best for anybody. Yes, some people may have had better lives than others but when life gives you lemons; make lemonade.

Growing up I formed an unconscious sense of entitlement. I felt any adult in my life owed me something because of my early abuse and neglect. I felt I should always get my way in every situation, right or wrong. I was always called spoiled. For a while I justified it and thought it was cute to be spoiled. This behavior carried over into my adult life.

What I didn't realize is I had grown to expect everyone I came into a relationship with to repair the damage that had been done to me. Once I began to change I became consciously aware of this behavior and corrected it. My husband is a true gentleman. He is affectionate, caring and verbal about how he feels about our relationship. When we were dating he would express his feelings to me regularly. I would give minimal feedback or responses.

I had come accustom to internalizing everything. I assumed he *knew* how I felt about him. One day we were at dinner and he told me he loved me. I instantly shut down. I got quiet and withdrew from the conversation. No matter what he said or did I would not respond.

Finally, I told him I did not play with that word. He assured me he wasn't playing and I assured him he didn't love me. After going back and forth for a few minutes I saw he was annoyed. I didn't really understand why until he asked me "Why won't you let me love you?" after a few minutes I responded "because I don't know how" WOW! That was a ton of bricks. For the first time in my life I had to face the fact I didn't know what love was or how to love.

It was at that moment I realized I was the only one who could fix my hurts.

I now know, it was not possible for anyone else to repair damage they did not cause. It was up to me to allow myself to heal; to accept the past and move on. My past had held me hostage long enough. The only way to move on was to let go of all of it. To let go is to simply acknowledge it, address it, when applicable, forgive it and move on. No it was not easy. It has taken years to reach this point. I kept working at it. My life has never been more fulfilling than it is today; because of ***letting go***.

This is the time you dig deeper within; more than ever before. Think about all the negative behaviors you have or allow in your atmosphere. At this point, you should be utilizing your quiet time more than ever.

    You have already started letting your walls down and are dealing with issues of your life. You are re-evaluating your relationships in all aspects. You are taking responsibility for all of your actions and making plans to move forward. Forgive those that have wronged you and ask for forgiveness for the ones you have wronged.

    Be open to **constructive** criticism from those that you know have your best interest at heart, such as your positive support team. When you feel the need to cry, yell, scream or shout do it! Get all the emotions out so you can began to feel again.

Often times we hear the saying "Let it go" and may think *that would be good if I knew how*. It is not easy to let go of anything; internally or externally. However, this journal writing will start the process.

Write about a past hurt in your life that you are ready to release.

_____

_____

_____

_____

_____

_____

_____

_____

_____

_____

_____

_____

_____

Continued

Write a letter to yourself allowing you to release yourself from the past hurt.

_____

_____

_____

_____

_____

_____

_____

_____

_____

_____

_____

_____

_____

_____

_____

_____

Continued

Write a letter to whoever caused this past hurt. In the letter be sure to forgive them thus release the past.

_____
_____
_____
_____
_____
_____
_____
_____
_____
_____
_____
_____
_____

repeat this journal step as often as you need to

Writing #10

Goals

Are you searching for a clue to what you want out of your life? Do you feel something has to change but you do not know what? I was in that very same predicament. It is important for you to take the time, right now, and decide what you want in your life; what you will and will not accept, what you will or will not do. It is time for you to make steadfast decisions, set some goals and boundaries in your life and stick to them.

When setting your goals be realistic and hone in on the skills you currently possess or that you will possess by furthering your learning; be it going back to school or self-study. **Goals are needed for direction.** The same concept applies to the boundaries you set.

If you say you are no longer dealing with a certain thing; then don't. You are no longer at liberty to continue to wander about in life being uncertain wishing for something to happen; you have to do it!

Set up for goals: Before you begin your list of goals and boundaries, take a little time to sit quietly and think. Write a list of your accomplishments. Write down everything from finishing high school, becoming a parent, getting your first job and so on. This will allow you to acknowledge the un-noticed success you have already attained. Okay, now you can go back to your goals and boundaries.

Goals are important. They are needed for direction.

Write one small goal for the next three weeks (one goal per week) and how you plan to reach the goal.

_____

_____

_____

_____

_____

_____

Continued

Write one larger goal for the next three months (one goal per month) and how you plan to reach the goal.

_____

_____

_____

_____

_____

_____

_____

_____

_____

_____

_____

_____

_____

_____

_____

_____

Continued

Write one goal to be reached in one year.

_____

_____

_____

_____

_____

_____

_____

_____

_____

_____

_____

_____

_____

Writing #11

Turning Point

I'm ok and I'm on my way – The turning point

By now you have climbed some steep hills. You have dealt with some major issues and uncovered things you were not even aware were there. You should be able to notice some of the old ways are gone; even if no one else points it out to you. I recall my turning point; when I noticed I wasn't the same and I was going to be okay.

My friend and I were in our favorite store. In the aisle over from us we could hear three or four young ladies being belligerent, cussing, laughing and talking loudly about some event they had attended. I instantly turned to my friend and said "OMG is that how I used to sound?"

She laughed and shook her head. I was floored. The revelation came to me right then; it was me all along. I always wanted others around me to change but the real issue was me.

I wanted others to change because I saw my faults illuminating in them. It was easier for me to say what *they* needed to do than to do a self-check and change me. Be mindful when someone wants you to change. It could possibly be themselves they see in you and vice versa. When you point the finger at someone else you have three pointed back at you.

When you are able to notice the old you in someone else you have jumped a major hurdle. It takes great humility to be able to recognize and acknowledge your own negativity. Be proud of yourself for growth and keep at your process.

At some time during your change process you will have noticed you no longer do or say some things as before.

Write two or three of your turning points in your process.

_____

_____

_____

_____

Writing #12

<u>Affirmations</u>

Build yourself up: Affirmations

An affirmation is a statement that provides emotional support or encouragement. Affirmations are necessary to assist you with uprooting the negative seeds that have planted over the years. They'll simultaneously drop positive seeds for new fruit to grow during your new harvest season.

*Your Self Esteem is all yours! It is how you feel about yourself. If you don't like you…change! Don't allow what someone else thinks about you affect how you feel about yourself. No one else can make you feel any kind of way about you.

During my change process I defined my affirmations as internal seeds planted to boost my self-esteem and help me begin to love me.

I chose and made up affirmations based on how I wanted to see myself and how I wanted to feel on the inside. The first affirmation I made up was of my name: Precious is – Patient, resilient, extraordinary, centered, imaginative, outgoing, understanding and successful. This is how I saw Precious although I was not there yet; I spoke it into existence. I said it aloud to plant the seed in my heart for future manifestation. Likewise, every day while getting dressed for work I would look in the mirror and say "You are too blessed to be stressed. You are a beautiful, smart, black woman and you deserve the best!" After saying this in the mirror, even when I didn't feel like it, I began to believe it. I began to say it all day. I didn't notice until a coworker asked me "Where did you get that from and why do you keep saying it".

I explained to her "by saying affirmations out loud, it goes through my ears and the seed is planted in my heart". The repetition of me saying it was the cultivation. That is the cycle of planting positive seed for harvest.

I also posted affirmations all over the house and on all the mirrors. The one in my bedroom stated: "You are a great mother, a hard worker and dedicated provider; you are going to be Okay". The bathroom's stated: "God loves you and I do too" (this was for me and my children). The kitchen's stated: "you are the best cook and your food is deliciously made with love." The one on the way out the door stated: "Smile beautiful; you can do all things through CHRIST that strengthens you".

Most of how you and I feel or have felt about ourselves is due to things that have been spoken. Words are powerful and may have been used to tear you down. Now you must use the same system to build yourself up. This time the words spoken will be positive.

Allow yourself to plant positive seed in your life. **You must be mindful of what is coming out of your mouth at all times**. It will go into your ears and be planted in your heart. After a while you will begin to see the fruit grow from the seeds you plant. Say your affirmations with **conviction and authority**.

Get full of yourself with the affirmations in the sense of *"Loving you some you"*. Once you master this technique you will begin to beam on the outside.

Affirmations and positive quotes will assist you greatly throughout your change process. They will help you to restore your self-esteem and plant positive seeds in your heart.

Ask yourself how you see yourself and create your name affirmation.

_____

_____

_____

_____

_____

_____

_____

_____

_____

Continued

Read and apply positive Affirmations and Quotes daily below are a few to start:

- ❖ In any situation, you can chose to be bitter or better.
- ❖ Smiles are contagious
- ❖ To get a different result you must apply a different action.
- ❖ Every failure is a step closer to your success.
- ❖ Forgiveness conditions your heart to move forward.
- ❖ I forgive those who have harmed me in my past and I am released.
- ❖ Accepting your past allows you to reach your future.
- ❖ I am full of energy and have an abundance of joy.
- ❖ My body is healthy; my mind is clear; my soul is at peace.
- ❖ I am above negative thinking and speaking.
- ❖ I will utilize my talents today so I can be extremely successful!
- ❖ I am bold enough to stand up for myself.

Without using the affirmations or quotes above write five affirmations and/or quotes to yourself to be repeated daily.

_____

_____

_____

_____

_____

_____

_____

_____

_____

_____

_____

_____

_____

_____

Reading

Reading stimulates the brain. It is a free fundamental activity available to mankind. Yet we utilize it the least. You will have to adjust your life a little more. Instead of watching television or hanging with your friends; read something of substance. It is a must that you retrain your brain to think positively. In doing so, you **must** read different types of literature.

Reading different types of books will not only help your mind grow and expand your vocabulary; it will also remove some of your boredom of reading. Visit the Library and get positive and wealth changing books. These are books that will enable you to challenge and change your way of thinking. It may take you a while to get accustomed to different types of reading but it will help your growth immensely.

You can find cheap books on Amazon.com or join a book club such as Doubleday book club on-line. If you are not an avid reader start reading 15 minutes a day and gradually move your time up. Before you know it reading will be your favorite past time. Below is a suggested reading list. If none suit you find some others that are more to your liking. The important thing is that you are reading to better yourself. It will help you in your future endeavors.

The Bible – any version

Battlefield of the Mind by Joyce Meyer

Sands to the Beach by Cloyd Kilgore Jr.

Reposition Yourself by T.D. Jakes

The total Money Makeover by Dave Ramsey

Discover the Power within You by Eric Butterworth

The Game of Life and How to Play it by Florence Scovel Shinn

The 5 Love Languages by Gary Chapman

Think and Grow Rich by Napoleon Hill

80 Proven ways to become a millionaire by Paul Damazo

I need your love – Is that true by Byron Katie

The Money Class & The Laws of Money by Suze Orman

The Lessons of Life by Suze Orman

The list is not all encompassing it is just to get you started. When reading you may want to have a reference books handy in case there are some things in the text you don't understand. You do not have to read just books. Open a magazine subscription such as Oprah, Vogue, or Reader's Digest. You can subscribe to US Weekly or NY Times. The important thing is that you are reading, expanding your brain power and taking in positive seeds.

Things to think about

Own your future, live up to your potential and change your life; starting today! From this moment forward believe in yourself to:

- ➢ Work on your changes every day.
- ➢ Work at being the best you that you can be.
- ➢ Have fun and enjoy your life every day.
- ➢ Choose to be happy no more excuses.

You may need to call on your support members to help hold you accountable. As of today, nothing else controls you but you.

*Note: If you are in an abusive relationship find a safe place to do this regularly. It is not easy to regain control of you when being abused. There are shelters in every city; find one!

Remember everything you do from this point on is to make you a better you. Choose to continue growing positively. When your growth process circle has become complete you will begin to walk in your purpose.

Bonus

Writing #13

What does love mean to you?

_____

_____

_____

_____

_____

_____

_____

_____

_____

_____

_____

_____

_____

_____

Inspiration keeps us motivated.

Who or what inspires you?

_____

_____

_____

_____

_____

_____

_____

_____

_____

_____

_____

_____

Relationships

Relationships are a part of life; some positive and some negative. We must make an effort to remove negative relationships from our immediate circle as quickly as possible.

Write about two or three toxic relationships in your life and how you can change them.

_____

_____

_____

_____

_____

_____

_____

_____

_____

_____

NOTES

www.ingramcontent.com/pod-product-compliance
Lightning Source LLC
Chambersburg PA
CBHW070101100426
42743CB00012B/2623